anythink

Guess What

CHERRY
LAKE
Publishing

Published in the United States of America by
Cherry Lake Publishing
Ann Arbor, Michigan
www.cherrylakepublishing.com

Content Adviser: Susan Heinrichs Gray
Reading Adviser: Marla Conn, ReadAbility, Inc.
Book Designer: Felicia Macheske

Photo Credits: © Opas Chotiphantawanon/Shutterstock Images, cover, 3, 7, 15, 16; © alexsvirid/Shutterstock Images, 1, 4:
© APaterson/Shutterstock Images, 9; © NatesPics/Shutterstock, 10; © Lone Wolf Photography/Shutterstock, 13; © Paul S. Wolf/
Shutterstock, 18; © KIM NGUYEN/Shutterstock, 21; © Andrey_Kuzmin/Shutterstock Images, back cover; © Eric Isselee/
Shutterstock Images, back cover

Copyright © 2016 by Cherry Lake Publishing
All rights reserved. No part of this book may be reproduced or utilized in any
form or by any means without written permission from the publisher.

Library of Congress Cataloging-in-Publication Data

Macheske, Felicia, author.
 Blue and bumpy : blue crab / Felicia Macheske.
  pages cm. — (Guess what)
  Summary: "Young children are natural problem solvers and always looking for answers, especially when it involves animals. Guess
What: Blue and Bumpy: Blue Crab provides young curious readers with striking visual clues and simply written hints. Using the
photos and text, readers rely on visual literacy skills, reading, and reasoning as they solve the animal mystery. Clearly written facts
give readers a deeper understanding of how the blue crab lives. Additional text features, including a glossary and an index, help
students locate information and learn new words"— Provided by publisher.
  Audience: K to grade 3.
  Includes index.
  ISBN 978-1-63470-717-6 (hardcover) — ISBN 978-1-63470-747-3 (pbk.) — ISBN 978-1-63470-732-9 (pdf) — ISBN 978-1-63470-762-6
(ebook)
 1. Blue crab—Juvenile literature. 2. Crabs—Juvenile literature. 3. Children's questions and answers. I. Title.
 QL444.M33M325 2016
 595.3'86—dc23
 2015026078

Cherry Lake Publishing would like to acknowledge the work of The Partnership for 21st Century Skills.
Please visit *www.p21.org* for more information.

Printed in the United States of America
Corporate Graphics

Table of Contents

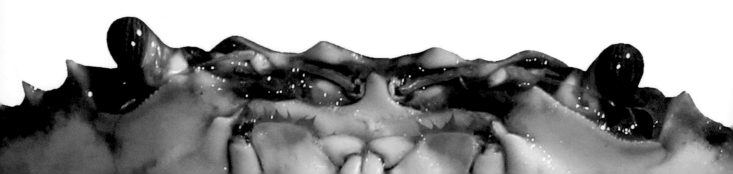

4

I have small eyes on top of my head.

I have claws that pinch.

Ouch!

My body is covered with a hard shell.

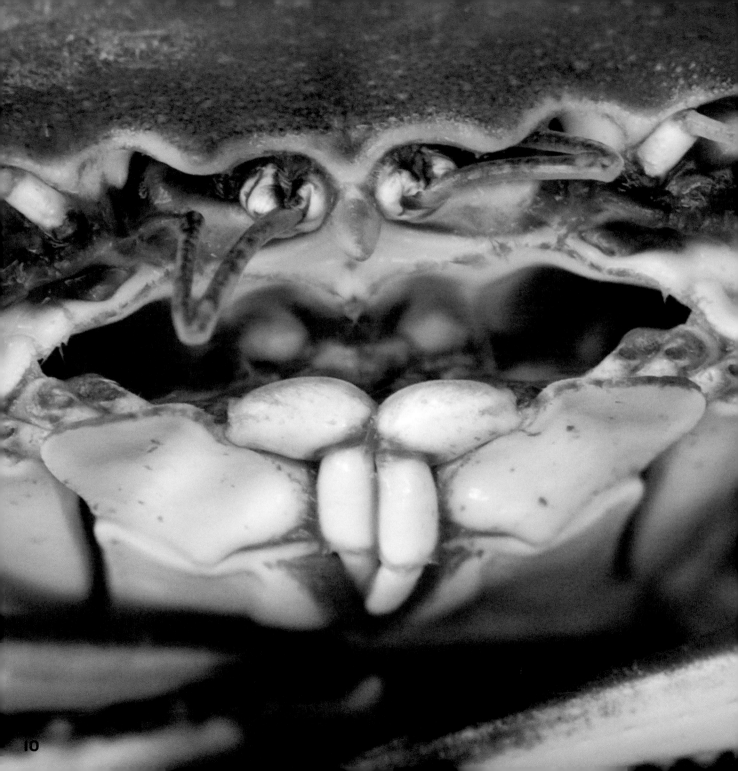

I use my mouthparts to eat many things.

I often live near the shore.

I have
many legs.

15

My back
legs are
shaped like
paddles.

Yikes!

Some other animals want to eat me.

Do you know what I am?

I'm a Blue Crab!

About Blue Crabs

1. Blue crabs feed on nearly anything they can find to eat.

2. The body of a blue crab is not actually blue. But its claws are.

3. Blue crabs usually walk sideways.

4. Blue crabs have a pair of legs that work like paddles. They help the crabs swim.

5. Blue crabs grow by **shedding** their shells. This is called molting.

Glossary

mouthparts (MOUTH-pahrts) the parts of an animal near the mouth that gather food

paddles (PAD-uhlz) broad, flat body parts that help an animal swim

shedding (SHED-ing) losing or getting rid of

Index